HEALING
AFFIRMATIONS
for Christian Black Women

A DAILY GUIDED JOURNAL

WITH PROMPTS TO SELF-REFLECT, GROW,

& BRING YOU CLOSER TO CHRIST

Inell Williams

HEALING
AFFIRMATIONS
for Christian Black Women

_____

_____

INTRODUCTION

Healing Affirmations for Christian Black Women is a powerful tool for spiritual growth and self-care. This journal is designed to provide daily inspiration and encouragement for black women who are seeking to deepen their relationship with God and improve their overall well-being.

In order to use this journal it is important to know: what exactly are affirmations? They are positive statements or declarations that are used to reprogram the mind and change negative thought patterns. They are a powerful tool for personal development and can help to improve self-esteem, boost confidence, and increase motivation.

This book covers 90 days of journaling with 90 different affirmations, many of which are specifically tailored to the unique experiences and challenges faced by Christian black women. From emphasizing self-acceptance and dealing with past traumas, to finding strength and resilience in Jesus during difficult times, the affirmations in this book are meant to help readers find healing and hope in their faith.

One of the key things that inspired me to create this journal is the notion that, as Christian Black women, we should remember that we are not alone in our struggles. The Bible reminds us that "God is our refuge and strength, a very present help in trouble" (Psalm 46:1, World English Bible). Whether you're a woman who is just starting your spiritual journey or someone who has been a Christian for many years, this book is the perfect tool for any black woman looking to deepen their relationship with God. As you put it to good use, remember that God is with you and will give you the strength and support to overcome any obstacle.

HOW TO USE

The affirmations in this journal are divided into these five sections:

- **Black Beauty, Self-Love, & Transformation**
- **Abundance, Charity, & Prosperity**
- **Friendship, Romance, & Relationships**
- **Forgiveness, Pain, & Happiness**
- **Women of the Bible, Femininity, & Womanhood**

You may go through all of the affirmations in order, or feel free to jump around from section to section everyday according to your changing needs.

Each page starts with a new affirmation. As you complete the "*Today I am grateful for...*" prompt, keep the affirmation at the top of the page in mind, or write what you're feeling in that moment. Then write your own affirmations in the space that reads "*I am...*". Again allow your affirmations to be inspired by the provided affirmation of the day. For "*Today's Positive Quote*" write one that resonates with you or uplifts you. This could be a Bible verse, a kind word or a piece of godly wisdom from someone in your life, or an inspirational quote that you saw on social media. Consider quoting a fellow Christian black woman whom you admire. No matter the source, pick a quote that you would like to look back on and keep within your memory.

Now write down your "*To Do List*" for the day. Allow the affirmation of the day to influence at least 1 of the items on your list. For example, if the affirmation is about self-care, at least one of the items on your to do list can focus on caring for yourself. Finish off your journaling for the day with a brief journal entry based on the affirmation of the day, or based on the topic of the section that you are on currently.

I take great care of myself, as *self-care* is next to godliness.

DATE __12/30/23__   M T W T F (S) S

Today I am grateful for...

my job, my good health, the beautiful weather today, and my dog who is my companion sent to me by God.

I am...

loved by many, especially Jesus. I am worthy, I am kind. I am hard working. I strive to be a better person.

TODAY'S POSITIVE QUOTE

"God said, 'Let's make man in our image, after our likeness.'"

Genesis 1:26, World English Bible

TO DO LIST

- ☑ Complete HW assignment
- ☐ ~~Meal prep~~
- ☑ *Self care meditation*
- ☐ Take down protective style
- ☐ Make Christian music playlist
- ☐
- ☐

JOURNAL ENTRY

God wants me to take care of myself because He made me like Him. I was made in His image, therefore I am important. I was feeling down and alone today, but after reflecting on God's love for me and doing some meditation I feel much better.

- Plan a self-care & prayer routine for myself tomorrow

My goals with this journal

Section 1:

BLACK BEAUTY, SELF-LOVE, & TRANSFORMATION

Many black women grew up experiencing a lack of representation, or were given messages - even by other black people - that blackness is physically inferior. As a result, some of us feel discontented about our hair, skin color, body, or facial features. You may or may not have experienced this yourself. This section is devoted to celebrating the distinct charm of black beauty and how its acceptance relates to our Creator.

Women of all backgrounds have a unique beauty bestowed upon their cultural group, by none other than God, and their beauty thus deserves to be cherished. As you focus on cherishing the unique beauty within yourself as a black woman, you'll discover a deeper understanding of God's grace and love. In this section of Healing Affirmations for Christian Black Women, you'll find affirmations that will help you build or maintain confidence in your black beauty and encourage self-care.

One thing that is important to remember is that beauty is not just skin-deep; one should strive towards building a rich inner beauty. Such beauty can be cultivated through a deepened relationship with Jesus, and with an earnest effort to become more like Him. God wants his work of art - that is, our outer appearance - to be appreciated and admired, but to a healthy extent of course, and not in a matter that moves us farther away from Him. Indeed "Charm is deceitful, and beauty is vain, but a woman who fears the Lord, she shall be praised" (Proverbs 31:30). Embrace your black beauty healthily and modestly, and let these affirmations guide you on your path to ever deeper self-love and transformation through the Lord Jesus Christ.

I am capable of deeply loving *myself,* just as God deeply loves me.

DATE _____   M T W T F S S

I am...

Today I am grateful for...

TODAY'S POSITIVE QUOTE

TO DO LIST

☐
☐
☐
☐
☐
☐
☐

_____

_____

_____

_____

_____

JOURNAL ENTRY

_____

_____

_____

_____

_____

_____

I strive to cultivate my *inner* and *outer* beauty through self-care and God's guidance.

DATE _____   M T W T F S S

I am...

Today I am grateful for...

TODAY'S POSITIVE QUOTE

TO DO LIST

- ☐
- ☐
- ☐
- ☐
- ☐
- ☐
- ☐

JOURNAL ENTRY

I am confident in my *black beauty.* God finds all of his people beautiful.

DATE _____   M T W T F S S

Today I am grateful for...

I am...

TODAY'S POSITIVE QUOTE

_____

_____

_____

_____

_____

TO DO LIST

- ☐
- ☐
- ☐
- ☐
- ☐
- ☐
- ☐

JOURNAL ENTRY

_____

_____

_____

_____

_____

_____

My unique beauty as a black woman - my hair, my skin and my body - is a reflection of God's divine *creativity.*

DATE _____   M T W T F S S

I am...

Today I am grateful for...

TODAY'S POSITIVE QUOTE

TO DO LIST

- ☐
- ☐
- ☐
- ☐
- ☐
- ☐
- ☐

JOURNAL ENTRY

_____

_____

_____

_____

_____

release negative thoughts and emotions, as I trust in God's power to *transform* me into an awe-inspiring black woman, *beautiful* in her surrender to the Lord!

DATE _____   M T W T F S S

I am...

Today I am grateful for...

TODAY'S POSITIVE QUOTE

TO DO LIST

- ☐
- ☐
- ☐
- ☐
- ☐
- ☐
- ☐

_____

_____

_____

_____

_____

JOURNAL ENTRY

I am beautiful in the eyes of the Lord and I will *embrace* my blackness.

DATE _____   M T W T F S S

I am...

Today I am grateful for...

TODAY'S POSITIVE QUOTE

TO DO LIST

- [ ]
- [ ]
- [ ]
- [ ]
- [ ]
- [ ]
- [ ]

JOURNAL ENTRY

I am worthy of self-love and self-care, as I was *wonderfully* and lovingly made by my Creator.

DATE _____ M T W T F S S

I am...

Today I am grateful for...

TODAY'S POSITIVE QUOTE

TO DO LIST

- ☐
- ☐
- ☐
- ☐
- ☐
- ☐
- ☐

JOURNAL ENTRY

_____

_____

_____

_____

_____

_____

I am confident in my skin! After all, it is the skin that my Lord gave me.

DATE _____   M T W T F S S

I am...

Today I am grateful for...

TODAY'S POSITIVE QUOTE

TO DO LIST

- [ ]
- [ ]
- [ ]
- [ ]
- [ ]
- [ ]
- [ ]

JOURNAL ENTRY

I am transformed by Christ's love. It *moves* through me and makes me a truly beautiful woman.

DATE _____ M T W T F S S

I am...

Today I am grateful for...

TODAY'S POSITIVE QUOTE

TO DO LIST

- ☐
- ☐
- ☐
- ☐
- ☐
- ☐
- ☐

JOURNAL ENTRY

I embrace my *unique* talents and qualities, internal and external, bestowed upon me from heaven.

DATE _____   M T W T F S S

I am...

Today I am grateful for...

TODAY'S POSITIVE QUOTE

TO DO LIST

- ☐
- ☐
- ☐
- ☐
- ☐
- ☐
- ☐

JOURNAL ENTRY

am lovable *because* I am created in God's image.

DATE _____   M T W T F S S

I am...

Today I am grateful for...

TODAY'S POSITIVE QUOTE

_____

_____

_____

_____

_____

_____

TO DO LIST

☐

☐

☐

☐

☐

☐

☐

JOURNAL ENTRY

_____

_____

_____

_____

_____

_____

God accepts and *loves* me unconditionally, and I should love myself likewise.

DATE _____   M T W T F S S

I am...

Today I am grateful for...

TODAY'S POSITIVE QUOTE

TO DO LIST

- [ ]
- [ ]
- [ ]
- [ ]
- [ ]
- [ ]
- [ ]

JOURNAL ENTRY

I celebrate my *blackness* just like God does.

DATE _____ M T W T F S S

I am...

Today I am grateful for...

TODAY'S POSITIVE QUOTE

TO DO LIST

- [ ]
- [ ]
- [ ]
- [ ]
- [ ]
- [ ]
- [ ]

JOURNAL ENTRY

I *radiate* self-love and positivity, as I am loved and cherished by God.

DATE _____   M T W T F S S

I am...

Today I am grateful for...

TODAY'S POSITIVE QUOTE

_____

_____

_____

_____

TO DO LIST

☐
☐
☐
☐
☐
☐
☐

JOURNAL ENTRY

_____

_____

_____

_____

_____

Because of *Jesus* **I am beautiful, powerful, and capable.**

DATE _____   M T W T F S S

I am...

Today I am grateful for...

TODAY'S POSITIVE QUOTE

TO DO LIST

☐
☐
☐
☐
☐
☐
☐

_____

_____

_____

_____

_____

JOURNAL ENTRY

_____

_____

_____

_____

_____

_____

My black beauty and grace are of God's *creation.*

DATE _____   M T W T F S S

I am...

Today I am grateful for...

TODAY'S POSITIVE QUOTE

TO DO LIST

- [ ]
- [ ]
- [ ]
- [ ]
- [ ]
- [ ]
- [ ]

JOURNAL ENTRY

I am *grateful* for the ways in which God continues to mold and shape me.

DATE _____   M T W T F S S

I am...

Today I am grateful for...

TODAY'S POSITIVE QUOTE

TO DO LIST

- [ ]
- [ ]
- [ ]
- [ ]
- [ ]
- [ ]
- [ ]

JOURNAL ENTRY

My body is a *temple*, and He wants me to care for myself. Sometimes this means prioritizing my own needs - after God - over other's.

DATE _____ M T W T F S S

I am...

Today I am grateful for...

TODAY'S POSITIVE QUOTE

TO DO LIST

- ☐
- ☐
- ☐
- ☐
- ☐
- ☐
- ☐

JOURNAL ENTRY

am *blessed* with the ability to overcome challenges and
change for the better, as I trust in God's strength and guidance.

DATE _____ M T W T F S S

I am...

Today I am grateful for...

TODAY'S POSITIVE QUOTE

TO DO LIST

- [ ]
- [ ]
- [ ]
- [ ]
- [ ]
- [ ]
- [ ]

JOURNAL ENTRY

I am valuable and *precious* in God's eyes, and thus worthy of self-improvement and self-love.

DATE _____   M T W T F S S

I am...

Today I am grateful for...

TODAY'S POSITIVE QUOTE

TO DO LIST

- [ ]
- [ ]
- [ ]
- [ ]
- [ ]
- [ ]
- [ ]

JOURNAL ENTRY

_____

_____

_____

_____

_____

_____

Adorned or natural *God* loves me.

DATE _____   M T W T F S S

I am...

Today I am grateful for...

TODAY'S POSITIVE QUOTE

_____
_____
_____
_____
_____

TO DO LIST

- ☐
- ☐
- ☐
- ☐
- ☐
- ☐
- ☐

JOURNAL ENTRY

_____
_____
_____
_____
_____
_____

Reflections

Section 2:

ABUNDANCE, CHARITY, & PROSPERITY

In this section you will delve into the realm of manifesting plenitude and fruitfulness. Our faith in Jesus can bring us a wealth of blessings, so long as we live righteously and are not afraid to ask for them, as "This is the confidence that we have in him, that, if we ask anything according to his will, he hears us" (1 John 5:14).

Prepare yourself for the rainfall of abundance that may descend upon you as a result of being a good disciple. But as you reap the rewards of your devotion, remember those who are in a less fortunate position compared to you. That is where charity comes in. There is a warm, fulfilling feeling that comes with being of service to others in the name of Jesus Christ. Charity does not have to be financial, though it may be an option depending on your circumstances. It can also mean sharing your time, your compassion, a warm smile, and putting your thoughts and energy into another person. On that note, ask yourself: what obstacles get in the way of black female prosperity, such as under-funded schools, unsafe neighborhoods, etc.? How can I contribute to the flourishing of other Christian black women, or black women in general? Sharing a kind word with black women you meet, supporting black female businesses and educational opportunities, and showing charity and thanksgiving to black women in your life who nutured you - a mother figure, teacher, neighbor, etc. - can be a good start.

The affirmations in this section aid you in fostering a positive, grateful mindset that will help you overcome any obstacle and bring your dreams to fruition. As you embrace abundance, charity, and prosperity always remember to trust in the grace of our Lord and Savior.

To me, fulfillment is the *sweet* fruit of charity.

DATE _____   M T W T F S S

I am...

Today I am grateful for...

TODAY'S POSITIVE QUOTE

TO DO LIST

- [ ]
- [ ]
- [ ]
- [ ]
- [ ]
- [ ]
- [ ]

JOURNAL ENTRY

With the Lord as my witness I *manifest* a life filled with joy, peace, and abundance.

DATE _____   M T W T F S S

I am...

Today I am grateful for...

TODAY'S POSITIVE QUOTE

TO DO LIST

- ☐
- ☐
- ☐
- ☐
- ☐
- ☐
- ☐

JOURNAL ENTRY

I am inspired that Jesus was *selfless* enough to die for my sins. Christ continues to show me the spirit of selflessness & charity in my life.

DATE _____   M T W T F S S

I am...

Today I am grateful for...

TODAY'S POSITIVE QUOTE

TO DO LIST

- ☐
- ☐
- ☐
- ☐
- ☐
- ☐
- ☐

JOURNAL ENTRY

can manifest a life with *happiness,* however I define that, as trust in God's plan for me.

DATE _____ M T W T F S S

Today I am grateful for...

I am...

TODAY'S POSITIVE QUOTE

_____

_____

_____

_____

_____

_____

TO DO LIST

- ☐
- ☐
- ☐
- ☐
- ☐
- ☐
- ☐

JOURNAL ENTRY

God's blessings gift me with the Christian *urge* to spread kindness, and to offer prayer in modest thanksgiving.

DATE _____   M T W T F S S

I am...

Today I am grateful for...

TODAY'S POSITIVE QUOTE

_____

_____

_____

_____

TO DO LIST

☐
☐
☐
☐
☐
☐
☐

JOURNAL ENTRY

_____

_____

_____

_____

_____

am worthy of being in good health and good spirits - physically and mentally. *I will* manifest it.

DATE _____   M T W T F S S

I am...

Today I am grateful for...

TODAY'S POSITIVE QUOTE

_____

_____

_____

_____

_____

TO DO LIST

- [ ]
- [ ]
- [ ]
- [ ]
- [ ]
- [ ]
- [ ]

JOURNAL ENTRY

_____

_____

_____

_____

_____

_____

I trust in *His* plan for my financial stability and abundance, as I am the child of a loving and generous God.

DATE _____   M T W T F S S

I am...

Today I am grateful for...

TODAY'S POSITIVE QUOTE

TO DO LIST

- ☐
- ☐
- ☐
- ☐
- ☐
- ☐
- ☐

JOURNAL ENTRY

I am *joyful* to act in service to loved ones and to those in need. May my service manifest even more joy in my life and in their's.

DATE _____   M T W T F S S

I am...

Today I am grateful for...

TODAY'S POSITIVE QUOTE

TO DO LIST

- [ ]
- [ ]
- [ ]
- [ ]
- [ ]
- [ ]
- [ ]

JOURNAL ENTRY

I can manifest a life of financial *peace* and freedom with God on my side.

DATE _____   M T W T F S S

I am...

Today I am grateful for...

TODAY'S POSITIVE QUOTE

TO DO LIST

- ☐
- ☐
- ☐
- ☐
- ☐
- ☐
- ☐

JOURNAL ENTRY

Jesus' guidance and wisdom can provide me with all of the prosperity I desire.

DATE _____   M T W T F S S

I am...

Today I am grateful for...

TODAY'S POSITIVE QUOTE

TO DO LIST

- [ ]
- [ ]
- [ ]
- [ ]
- [ ]
- [ ]
- [ ]

_____

_____

_____

_____

JOURNAL ENTRY

_____

_____

_____

_____

_____

Positivity, hard work, and *faith* are the vehicles of success.

DATE _____   M T W T F S S

I am...

Today I am grateful for...

TODAY'S POSITIVE QUOTE

TO DO LIST

- ☐
- ☐
- ☐
- ☐
- ☐
- ☐
- ☐

JOURNAL ENTRY

I am made content by sharing with and thinking of others in a *Christ-like* **manner. May my charitable actions bless my future and my present.**

DATE _____ M T W T F S S

I am...

Today I am grateful for...

TODAY'S POSITIVE QUOTE

TO DO LIST

- [ ]
- [ ]
- [ ]
- [ ]
- [ ]
- [ ]
- [ ]

JOURNAL ENTRY

God will provide.

DATE _____ M T W T F S S

I am...

Today I am grateful for...

TODAY'S POSITIVE QUOTE

_____

_____

_____

_____

_____

TO DO LIST

☐
☐
☐
☐
☐
☐
☐

JOURNAL ENTRY

_____

_____

_____

_____

_____

_____

Jesus knows my *worth*, and I know it too.

DATE _____   M T W T F S S

I am...

Today I am grateful for...

TODAY'S POSITIVE QUOTE

TO DO LIST

- ☐
- ☐
- ☐
- ☐
- ☐
- ☐
- ☐

JOURNAL ENTRY

I have a heart full of *gratitude* and a mind set on positivity, which will help me make my dreams a reality.

DATE _____ M T W T F S S

I am...

Today I am grateful for...

TODAY'S POSITIVE QUOTE

TO DO LIST

☐
☐
☐
☐
☐
☐
☐

JOURNAL ENTRY

With Jesus I shall prosper *tenfold.*

DATE _____ M T W T F S S

I am...

Today I am grateful for...

TODAY'S POSITIVE QUOTE

TO DO LIST

- ☐
- ☐
- ☐
- ☐
- ☐
- ☐
- ☐

JOURNAL ENTRY

Reflections

Section 3:

FRIENDSHIP, ROMANCE, & RELATIONSHIPS

This section explores the significance of positive relationships in our lives and how they can positively impact our mental and emotional well-being. The right people can help fortify our relationship with Christ. A supportive network of friends and loved ones can bring comfort and uplift us in difficult times, and can work as a team to remind one another to stay on the path of righteousness, as "Two are better than one, because they have a good reward for their labor. For if they fall, the one will lift up his companion. But woe to him who is alone when he falls, for he has no one to help him up" (Ecclesiastes 4:9-10).

The affirmations in this section are meant to help you discover the importance of having healthy boundaries and avoiding toxic relationships, which can drain and harm us. Look at them as an opportunity to reflect upon the healing power of love and how it can be a source of comfort and guidance.

God's love for us is unconditional and unchanging, and we can bring that love into our relationships with others. By seeking to build Christ-like relationships, we can uplift and support one another, providing a source of healing and companionship that is truly holy. So, let us cherish our relationships, cultivate supportive networks, and enjoy the uplifting effects of healthy and godly relationships in all areas of our life.

I am worthy of a loving and *healthy* romantic relationship, as God created me for connection.

DATE _____   M T W T F S S

I am...

Today I am grateful for...

TODAY'S POSITIVE QUOTE

TO DO LIST

- [ ]
- [ ]
- [ ]
- [ ]
- [ ]
- [ ]
- [ ]

JOURNAL ENTRY

I have or will have strong and *supportive* **friendships in my life, in accordance to God's will.**

DATE _____   M T W T F S S

I am...

Today I am grateful for...

TODAY'S POSITIVE QUOTE

TO DO LIST

- [ ]
- [ ]
- [ ]
- [ ]
- [ ]
- [ ]
- [ ]

JOURNAL ENTRY

I am capable of healing from toxic experiences with friends, family, and/or partners. They will not keep me from the path of *righteousness.*

DATE _____   M T W T F S S

I am...

Today I am grateful for...

TODAY'S POSITIVE QUOTE

TO DO LIST

- ☐
- ☐
- ☐
- ☐
- ☐
- ☐
- ☐

JOURNAL ENTRY

see *God's face* in my close circle.

DATE _____ M T W T F S S

I am...

Today I am grateful for...

TODAY'S POSITIVE QUOTE

TO DO LIST

- ☐
- ☐
- ☐
- ☐
- ☐
- ☐
- ☐

JOURNAL ENTRY

My *value* **as a woman is not defined by the color of my skin, as God made no skin color superior to another. A** *truly* **godly man recognizes this.**

DATE _____ M T W T F S S

I am...

Today I am grateful for...

TODAY'S POSITIVE QUOTE

TO DO LIST

- [ ]
- [ ]
- [ ]
- [ ]
- [ ]
- [ ]
- [ ]

JOURNAL ENTRY

The Lord wants me to be surrounded by people who *uplift* me.

DATE _____ M T W T F S S

I am...

Today I am grateful for...

TODAY'S POSITIVE QUOTE

TO DO LIST

- ☐
- ☐
- ☐
- ☐
- ☐
- ☐
- ☐

_____
_____
_____
_____
_____

JOURNAL ENTRY

_____
_____
_____
_____
_____
_____

My relationship with the *Lord Almighty* supersedes all others.

DATE _____   M T W T F S S

I am...

Today I am grateful for...

TODAY'S POSITIVE QUOTE

_____

_____

_____

_____

TO DO LIST

- ☐
- ☐
- ☐
- ☐
- ☐
- ☐
- ☐

JOURNAL ENTRY

_____

_____

_____

_____

_____

_____

A godly man provides for me, protects me, and leads a relationship. God created us to *complement* one another.

DATE _____ M T W T F S S

I am...

Today I am grateful for...

TODAY'S POSITIVE QUOTE

_____
_____
_____
_____
_____
_____

TO DO LIST

- ☐
- ☐
- ☐
- ☐
- ☐
- ☐
- ☐

JOURNAL ENTRY

_____
_____
_____
_____
_____
_____

I am capable of setting and maintaining *healthy* boundaries in my relationships with friends, my romantic partner, and family.

DATE _____   M T W T F S S

I am...

Today I am grateful for...

TODAY'S POSITIVE QUOTE

_____

_____

_____

_____

TO DO LIST

☐

☐

☐

☐

☐

☐

☐

JOURNAL ENTRY

_____

_____

_____

_____

_____

I am, or will be with, a *God-fearing* man who lifts me up and supports me in my journey of faith.

DATE _____ M T W T F S S

I am...

Today I am grateful for...

TODAY'S POSITIVE QUOTE

TO DO LIST

- ☐
- ☐
- ☐
- ☐
- ☐
- ☐
- ☐

JOURNAL ENTRY

I am *unafraid* to rethink friendships and other relationships with people who hold me back mentally, emotionally, or spiritually.

DATE _____ M T W T F S S

I am...

Today I am grateful for...

TODAY'S POSITIVE QUOTE

TO DO LIST

- ☐
- ☐
- ☐
- ☐
- ☐
- ☐
- ☐

JOURNAL ENTRY

God breathes *love* into my relationships.

DATE _____   M T W T F S S

I am...

Today I am grateful for...

TODAY'S POSITIVE QUOTE

TO DO LIST

- ☐
- ☐
- ☐
- ☐
- ☐
- ☐
- ☐

JOURNAL ENTRY

Toxic people are blessings in disguise. God sent them to bestow me with strength and *wisdom.*

DATE _____   M T W T F S S

I am...

Today I am grateful for...

TODAY'S POSITIVE QUOTE

TO DO LIST

- ☐
- ☐
- ☐
- ☐
- ☐
- ☐
- ☐

JOURNAL ENTRY

Even without a friend, partner, or family I am *not alone,* for God is with me.

DATE _____   M T W T F S S

I am...

Today I am grateful for...

TODAY'S POSITIVE QUOTE

TO DO LIST

- [ ]
- [ ]
- [ ]
- [ ]
- [ ]
- [ ]
- [ ]

_____

_____

_____

_____

_____

JOURNAL ENTRY

_____

_____

_____

_____

_____

_____

I strive to ensure that all of the relationships in my life *reflect* the relationship I have with Jesus.

DATE _____ M T W T F S S

I am...

Today I am grateful for...

TODAY'S POSITIVE QUOTE

TO DO LIST

- [ ]
- [ ]
- [ ]
- [ ]
- [ ]
- [ ]
- [ ]

JOURNAL ENTRY

_____

_____

_____

_____

_____

_____

God knew me before I was born. His relationship with me is *unmatched.*

DATE _____   M T W T F S S

I am...

Today I am grateful for...

TODAY'S POSITIVE QUOTE

TO DO LIST

- [ ]
- [ ]
- [ ]
- [ ]
- [ ]
- [ ]
- [ ]

JOURNAL ENTRY

Good friends and good neighbors *pray* for one another.

DATE _____ M T W T F S S

I am...

Today I am grateful for...

TODAY'S POSITIVE QUOTE

_____

_____

_____

_____

TO DO LIST

- ☐
- ☐
- ☐
- ☐
- ☐
- ☐
- ☐

JOURNAL ENTRY

_____

_____

_____

_____

_____

_____

True friends are a blessing, *praise* the Lord.

DATE _____ M T W T F S S

I am...

Today I am grateful for...

TODAY'S POSITIVE QUOTE

_____
_____
_____
_____
_____

TO DO LIST

- [ ]
- [ ]
- [ ]
- [ ]
- [ ]
- [ ]
- [ ]

JOURNAL ENTRY

_____
_____
_____
_____
_____
_____

God is pure and God is good. Distancing myself from toxicity only brings me *closer* to Him.

DATE _____   M T W T F S S

I am...

Today I am grateful for...

TODAY'S POSITIVE QUOTE

TO DO LIST

- ☐
- ☐
- ☐
- ☐
- ☐
- ☐
- ☐

JOURNAL ENTRY

Reflections

Section 4:

FORGIVENESS, PAIN, & HAPPINESS

The journey to true happiness and inner peace often requires confronting and healing past pain and hurt. As a Christian black woman you may or may not have experienced misogynoir and personally know its effects on your mental and spiritual well-being, or have seen the influence of misogynoir on other black women, along with other personal hardships specific to you as an individual. In this section I challenge you to look at past tribulations, especially those caused by others, with an open heart and clemency. It can be a difficult mindset to take on, but it is a challenge worth taking on as forgiveness has the power to liberate your mind and soul. We are called to forgive not just others but ourselves as well, and to allow the love of God and the guidance of Jesus to heal our wounds.

Here you will explore the transformative power of forgiveness in your life. Like Paul emphasizes in Colossians 3:13, "Bear with each other, and forgive each other. If someone has something against you, forgive him, so that also God in Christ may forgive you your trespasses." Through your affirmations learn to let go of resentment and disappointment, and embrace the divine wisdom and growth that comes from forgiveness. Earnestly embark upon this journey of forgiveness to experience the true joy and freedom that come from a heart filled with mercy and love.

am worthy of forgiveness, and I will *forgive* myself, just as
God forgives me.

DATE _____   M T W T F S S

I am...

Today I am grateful for...

TODAY'S POSITIVE QUOTE

_____

_____

_____

_____

_____

TO DO LIST

☐

☐

☐

☐

☐

☐

☐

JOURNAL ENTRY

_____

_____

_____

_____

_____

_____

_____

I am blessed with the *gift* of healing and I trust in God's power to heal me.

DATE _____ M T W T F S S

Today I am grateful for...

I am...

TODAY'S POSITIVE QUOTE

_____

_____

_____

_____

TO DO LIST

- ☐
- ☐
- ☐
- ☐
- ☐
- ☐
- ☐

JOURNAL ENTRY

_____

_____

_____

_____

_____

_____

I am grateful for the healing and *growth* that comes from past struggles.

DATE _____   M T W T F S S

I am...

Today I am grateful for...

TODAY'S POSITIVE QUOTE

TO DO LIST

- ☐
- ☐
- ☐
- ☐
- ☐
- ☐
- ☐

JOURNAL ENTRY

God sees my pain - past, present, and future - and my healing is in *His plan.*

DATE _____ M T W T F S S

I am...

Today I am grateful for...

TODAY'S POSITIVE QUOTE

TO DO LIST

- ☐
- ☐
- ☐
- ☐
- ☐
- ☐
- ☐

JOURNAL ENTRY

Time has the power to mend *all* of my wounds. God has made it so.

DATE _____   M T W T F S S

I am...

Today I am grateful for...

TODAY'S POSITIVE QUOTE

TO DO LIST

- [ ]
- [ ]
- [ ]
- [ ]
- [ ]
- [ ]
- [ ]

JOURNAL ENTRY

In this life we all have a cross to bear. *I can* **bear my cross just as Jesus bore his.**

DATE _____ M T W T F S S

I am...

Today I am grateful for...

TODAY'S POSITIVE QUOTE

TO DO LIST

- [ ]
- [ ]
- [ ]
- [ ]
- [ ]
- [ ]
- [ ]

JOURNAL ENTRY

In the midst of my struggles Jesus *is there* for me.

DATE _____   M T W T F S S

I am...

Today I am grateful for...

TODAY'S POSITIVE QUOTE

TO DO LIST

☐
☐
☐
☐
☐
☐
☐

JOURNAL ENTRY

I trust in Christ's guidance and *protection* during hard times.

DATE _____   M T W T F S S

I am...

Today I am grateful for...

TODAY'S POSITIVE QUOTE

_____

_____

_____

_____

TO DO LIST

- ☐
- ☐
- ☐
- ☐
- ☐
- ☐
- ☐

JOURNAL ENTRY

_____

_____

_____

_____

_____

_____

God *will* lead me to happier days.

DATE _____ M T W T F S S

I am...

Today I am grateful for...

TODAY'S POSITIVE QUOTE

TO DO LIST

_____

_____

☐

_____

☐

_____

☐

_____

☐

_____

☐

_____

☐

☐

JOURNAL ENTRY

_____

_____

_____

_____

_____

_____

_____

In times of pain and disappointment, I *look* to God.

DATE _____ M T W T F S S

I am...

Today I am grateful for...

TODAY'S POSITIVE QUOTE

TO DO LIST

- ☐
- ☐
- ☐
- ☐
- ☐
- ☐
- ☐

JOURNAL ENTRY

_____

_____

_____

_____

_____

_____

need not *forget* trespasses, but I can forgive them at my own
pace.

DATE _____   M T W T F S S

I am...

Today I am grateful for...

TODAY'S POSITIVE QUOTE

TO DO LIST

- ☐
- ☐
- ☐
- ☐
- ☐
- ☐
- ☐

JOURNAL ENTRY

_____

_____

_____

_____

_____

_____

I am capable of overcoming any pain through the *power* of Jesus that resides within me.

DATE _____   M T W T F S S

I am...

Today I am grateful for...

TODAY'S POSITIVE QUOTE

TO DO LIST

- [ ]
- [ ]
- [ ]
- [ ]
- [ ]
- [ ]
- [ ]

JOURNAL ENTRY

am *growing* and transforming even amidst hardship.

DATE _____   M T W T F S S

I am...

Today I am grateful for...

TODAY'S POSITIVE QUOTE

TO DO LIST

- [ ]
- [ ]
- [ ]
- [ ]
- [ ]
- [ ]
- [ ]

JOURNAL ENTRY

Pain and heartache make me a wiser Christian and a *stronger* disciple.

DATE _____ 　M　T　W　T　F　S　S

I am...

Today I am grateful for...

TODAY'S POSITIVE QUOTE

TO DO LIST

- [ ]
- [ ]
- [ ]
- [ ]
- [ ]
- [ ]
- [ ]

_____

_____

_____

_____

JOURNAL ENTRY

_____

_____

_____

_____

_____

_____

God is a source of *comfort* for me during times of uncertainty.

DATE _____   M T W T F S S

I am...

Today I am grateful for...

TODAY'S POSITIVE QUOTE

TO DO LIST

- ☐
- ☐
- ☐
- ☐
- ☐
- ☐
- ☐

_____

_____

_____

_____

_____

JOURNAL ENTRY

_____

_____

_____

_____

_____

_____

Every battle I face is God sharing a piece of His *divine* wisdom with me.

DATE _____   M T W T F S S

I am...

Today I am grateful for...

TODAY'S POSITIVE QUOTE

_____

_____

_____

_____

TO DO LIST

☐
☐
☐
☐
☐
☐
☐

JOURNAL ENTRY

_____

_____

_____

_____

_____

_____

Reflections

WOMEN OF THE BIBLE, FEMININITY, & WOMANHOOD

Various women in the Bible embody traits of strength, grace, resilience and femininity. Many of us can see ourselves reflected in their stories, and they can serve as a great source of inspiration for Christian black women.

As Proverbs 31:25 states, "Strength and honor are her clothing. She shall rejoice in time to come," the admirable inner force and uprightness of women can inspire others to proudly embrace their womanhood and act as a beacon of righteousness for those around them.

Through this set of affirmations we will explore the image of God within us as women, the beauty of femininity, and the power of womanhood. This section includes a bit of Bible study. Use it to familiarize yourself with women of the Bible such as Mary of Nazareth, Ruth, and Esther, and find inspiration in their journeys of devotion, grace, and love. Feel free to watch videos, read Bible passages and use other means of studying the women of the Bible and the lessons that can be learned from them.

The last two affirmations of the day have blank spaces for writing in your own personal examples of women whom you admire. These affirmations will help us embrace our divine nature, our worth, our softness, and remind us that as daughters of Christ, we should strive to be shining examples of God's love and holiness.

I am confident in my own femininity as it is a reflection of God's own beauty and *love* for womankind.

DATE _____   M T W T F S S

Today I am grateful for...

I am...

TODAY'S POSITIVE QUOTE

_____
_____
_____
_____
_____
_____

TO DO LIST

- ☐
- ☐
- ☐
- ☐
- ☐
- ☐
- ☐

JOURNAL ENTRY

_____
_____
_____
_____
_____
_____
_____

I am a woman of *God,* so I will not be defined by earthly standards, but by heavenly ones.

DATE _____   M T W T F S S

I am...

Today I am grateful for...

TODAY'S POSITIVE QUOTE

TO DO LIST

- ☐
- ☐
- ☐
- ☐
- ☐
- ☐
- ☐

JOURNAL ENTRY

have or will have *admirable* and uplifting female role models n my life who reflect God's wisdom and grace.

DATE _____   M T W T F S S

I am...

Today I am grateful for...

TODAY'S POSITIVE QUOTE

TO DO LIST

- ☐
- ☐
- ☐
- ☐
- ☐
- ☐
- ☐

JOURNAL ENTRY

I am *beautiful* in the eyes of God and will not compare myself to others.

DATE _____   M T W T F S S

Today I am grateful for...

I am...

TODAY'S POSITIVE QUOTE

_____

_____

_____

_____

TO DO LIST

☐
☐
☐
☐
☐
☐
☐

JOURNAL ENTRY

_____

_____

_____

_____

_____

_____

honor **and emulate the strength and faith of women like Mary of Nazareth in my own life.**

DATE _____   M T W T F S S

I am...

Today I am grateful for...

TODAY'S POSITIVE QUOTE

TO DO LIST

- [ ]
- [ ]
- [ ]
- [ ]
- [ ]
- [ ]
- [ ]

_____

_____

_____

_____

JOURNAL ENTRY

_____

_____

_____

_____

_____

_____

I strive to embody the selflessness and *kindness* of women like Ruth in my relationships and actions.

DATE _____   M T W T F S S

I am...

Today I am grateful for...

TODAY'S POSITIVE QUOTE

TO DO LIST

- ☐
- ☐
- ☐
- ☐
- ☐
- ☐
- ☐

_____

_____

_____

_____

JOURNAL ENTRY

_____

_____

_____

_____

_____

_____

am proud of the *softness* and vulnerability that comes with being a woman, as it a reflection of God's own love and compassion.

DATE _____   M T W T F S S

I am...

Today I am grateful for...

TODAY'S POSITIVE QUOTE

_____

_____

_____

_____

_____

_____

TO DO LIST

- [ ]
- [ ]
- [ ]
- [ ]
- [ ]
- [ ]
- [ ]

JOURNAL ENTRY

_____

_____

_____

_____

_____

_____

_____

I draw strength from the *perseverance* and grace of women like Mary Magdalene in my own struggles.

DATE _____   M T W T F S S

I am...

Today I am grateful for...

TODAY'S POSITIVE QUOTE

TO DO LIST

- [ ]
- [ ]
- [ ]
- [ ]
- [ ]
- [ ]
- [ ]

JOURNAL ENTRY

can choose to live in the image of women like Priscilla, who are great leaders and have a *deep* relationship with God.

DATE _____   M T W T F S S

I am...

Today I am grateful for...

TODAY'S POSITIVE QUOTE

TO DO LIST

- ☐
- ☐
- ☐
- ☐
- ☐
- ☐
- ☐

JOURNAL ENTRY

I am a daughter of the Lord *Jesus Christ,* and I walk in the authority he has given me.

DATE _____   M T W T F S S

Today I am grateful for...

I am...

TODAY'S POSITIVE QUOTE

_____

_____

_____

_____

TO DO LIST

☐
☐
☐
☐
☐
☐
☐

JOURNAL ENTRY

_____

_____

_____

_____

_____

_____

draw inspiration from the resilience and *courage* of women like Esther in facing my own challenges.

DATE _____ M T W T F S S

I am...

Today I am grateful for...

TODAY'S POSITIVE QUOTE

TO DO LIST

- [ ]
- [ ]
- [ ]
- [ ]
- [ ]
- [ ]
- [ ]

JOURNAL ENTRY

God made me feminine in a way that resembles and also differs from other women's femininity. My femininity is *unique* to me.

DATE _____ M T W T F S S

I am...

Today I am grateful for...

TODAY'S POSITIVE QUOTE

_____

_____

_____

_____

TO DO LIST

☐
☐
☐
☐
☐
☐
☐

JOURNAL ENTRY

_____

_____

_____

_____

_____

_____

draw inspiration from the determination and *strength* of women like Jael in facing my own challenges.

DATE _____   M T W T F S S

I am...

Today I am grateful for...

TODAY'S POSITIVE QUOTE

TO DO LIST

☐

☐

☐

☐

☐

☐

☐

JOURNAL ENTRY

I draw strength from the faith and *devotion* of women like Hannah in my own relationship with God.

DATE _____   M T W T F S S

I am...

Today I am grateful for...

TODAY'S POSITIVE QUOTE

TO DO LIST

- [ ]
- [ ]
- [ ]
- [ ]
- [ ]
- [ ]
- [ ]

JOURNAL ENTRY

Eve *herself* was African.

DATE _____   M T W T F S S

I am...

Today I am grateful for...

TODAY'S POSITIVE QUOTE

TO DO LIST

- [ ]
- [ ]
- [ ]
- [ ]
- [ ]
- [ ]
- [ ]

JOURNAL ENTRY

As a black woman my *identity* is in Christ before all else.

DATE _____   M T W T F S S

I am...

Today I am grateful for...

TODAY'S POSITIVE QUOTE

TO DO LIST

- [ ]
- [ ]
- [ ]
- [ ]
- [ ]
- [ ]
- [ ]

JOURNAL ENTRY

I draw *inspiration* **from women like** _____
for my own journey as a Christian.

DATE _____   M T W T F S S

I am...

Today I am grateful for...

TODAY'S POSITIVE QUOTE

TO DO LIST

☐
☐
☐
☐
☐
☐
☐

JOURNAL ENTRY

I draw *inspiration* from women like _____
for my own journey as a God-fearing black woman.

DATE _____   M T W T F S S

I am...

Today I am grateful for...

TODAY'S POSITIVE QUOTE

TO DO LIST

- ☐
- ☐
- ☐
- ☐
- ☐
- ☐
- ☐

JOURNAL ENTRY

Reflections

34722768R00062